Power Words!

Color Your Way to a Better Vocabulary

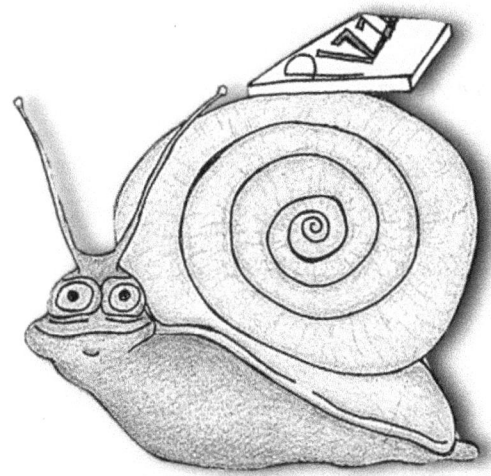

O. B. Radley

Power Words!

Color Your Way to a Better Vocabulary

Printed in the United States of America

First Printing: 2020

ISBN: 978-1-952674-10-5

Publisher: LeRoy Mac Publishing Ho

LeROY•MaC
PUBLISHING HOUSE

Name:_____

O. B. Radley

Word List

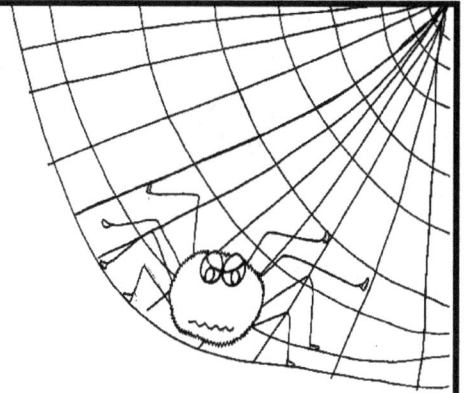

Abrogate- cancel, deny, appeal.

(ab-ruh-gate)

Paul the potato had to <u>abrogate</u> his plans to run a marathon. His new television arrived earlier than expected.

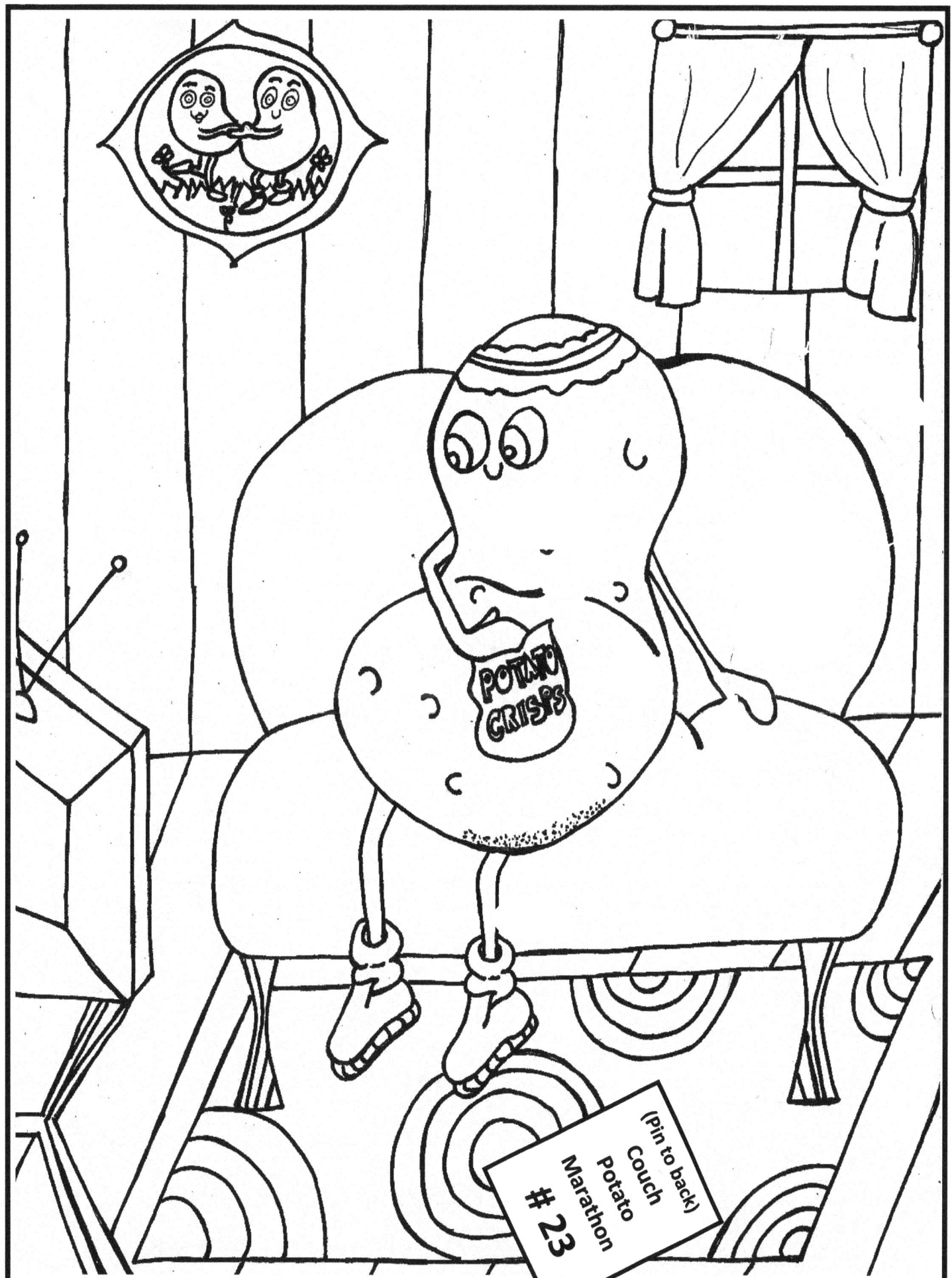

POTATO CRISPS

(Pin to back)
Couch
Potato
Marathon
23

Conducive- to be suitable for; able to bring about.

(kuh *n*-**doo**-siv)

- Howler Monkeys are NOT <u>conducive</u> to a quiet library experience.

These worms changing into butterflies are really scary! Definitely not conductive for reading to children! Not suitable at all! Whoop! WHOOP! WHOOP! WHOOP!
Glad we didn't ask him to read the one about the baby sharks!

Cacophony- a harsh or chaotic mixture of sounds.

(kuh-kof-uh-nee)

-Denny was fearful and annoyed at the cacophony the closet band made.

Assiduous- persistent; hardworking.

(uh-sij-oo-uhs)

-You will find that a tiger can be a most <u>assiduous</u> butcher.

Ebullient- joyously unrestrained.
(ih-**buhl**-y*uh* nt)

- The big, pink blob was in an <u>ebullient</u> mood on the first day of school.

Buttress- to support, to prop up.
(**buh**-tris)

-Lily had to <u>buttress</u> her tent after the cat and dog storm.

Exacerbate- to increase severity; to make worse.

(ig-**zas**-er-beyt)

-The new stylist only served to <u>exacerbate</u> Polly the Poodle's fluff.

Austere- severe, strict, stern in appearance or manner.

(aw-steer)

Mable Spider is very austere protecting her priceless work of art.

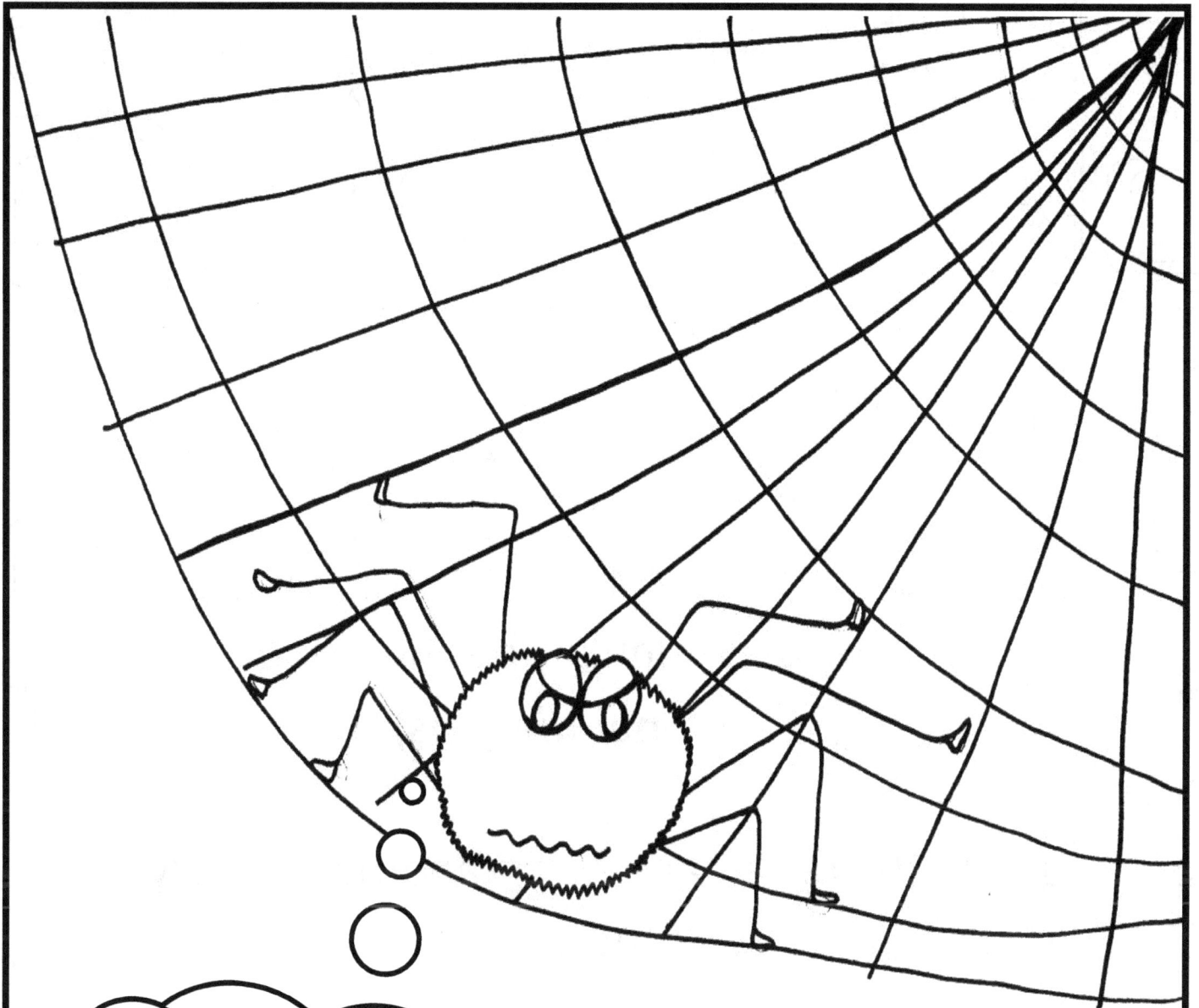

Pesky flies are always getting too close to my beautiful web. They don't understand the effort it took to make this.

Analogous- similar, but not identical.
(*uh*-**nal**-*uh*-g*uh*s)

- Jenny the rabbit and her grandma are very <u>analogous</u> to each other.

Analogous Disco Night!
Dress Like Twins!

22

© Copyright 2020 OBRadley

Discomfit- cause to lose one's composure; to frustrate the plans of.
(dis-**kuhm**-fit)

- Alex was <u>discomfit</u> after learning his pizza was being delivered by a snail.

SNAIL pizza! I can't believe it. I thought the ad said Swell Pizza. I will probably have to wait another thirty minutes!
This job is so much better than the coffee shop. Trying to remember all those flavors was such a discomfit for me. This is so peaceful! I'll be at my first house in just two hours.

Mendacious- given or prone to lying.
(men-**dey**-sh*uhs*)

- Megan gave a <u>mendacious</u> excuse to the teacher as to where her homework went.

Flagitious- criminal, villainous.
(fl*uh*-**jish**-*uh* s)

-Larenda the Cow protested what he deems the
<u>flagitious</u> consumption of beef.

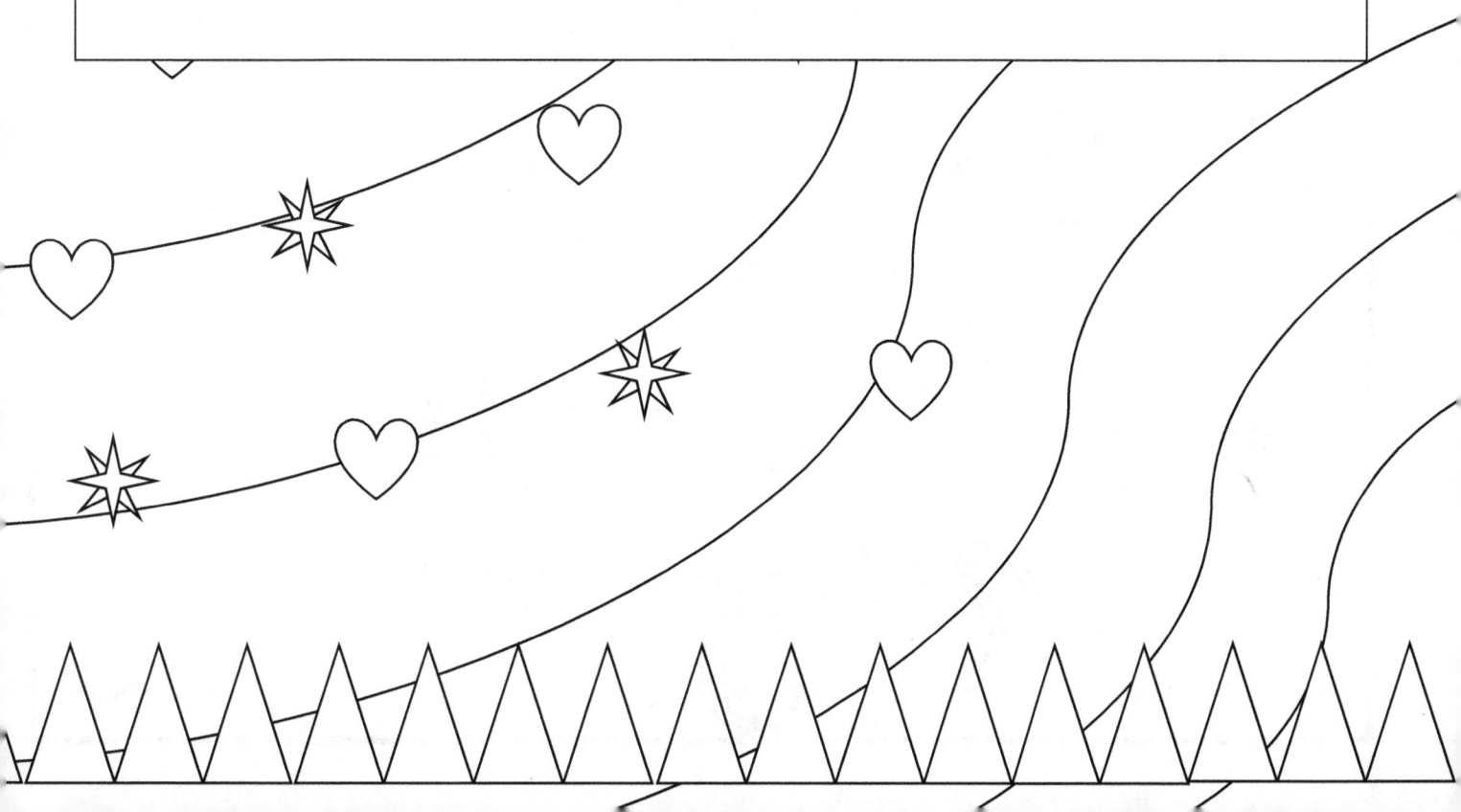

Pulchritudinous- having great physical beauty.

(puhl-kri-**tood**-n-*uh* s)

- Sally will be the most <u>pulchritudinous</u> orange in Orange City with the use of her new peeler.

Quixotic- exceedingly idealistic; unrealistic and impractical.

(kwik-**sot**-ik)

-Carl's idea that he could eat as many carrots as he wanted without turning orange was very quixotic.

How dare this petulant child try to eat me! I have been dry aged longer than she's been alive!

Petulant- cranky, pouty, irritable.
(**pech**-*uh*-l*uh*nt)

-Sam the steak gets <u>petulant</u> when anyone tries to eat him for dinner.

Sagacity- wisdom.
(*suh*-**gas-i-tee**)

- By the third hour of the lecture the students had fallen asleep. Thus, missing out on all the <u>sagacity</u> Professor Sloth had to offer.

Vociferous- conspicuously and offensively loud.

(voh-**sif**-er-*uh*s)

- Gwen the car sped down the street in a <u>vociferous</u> manner, waking up the whole town.

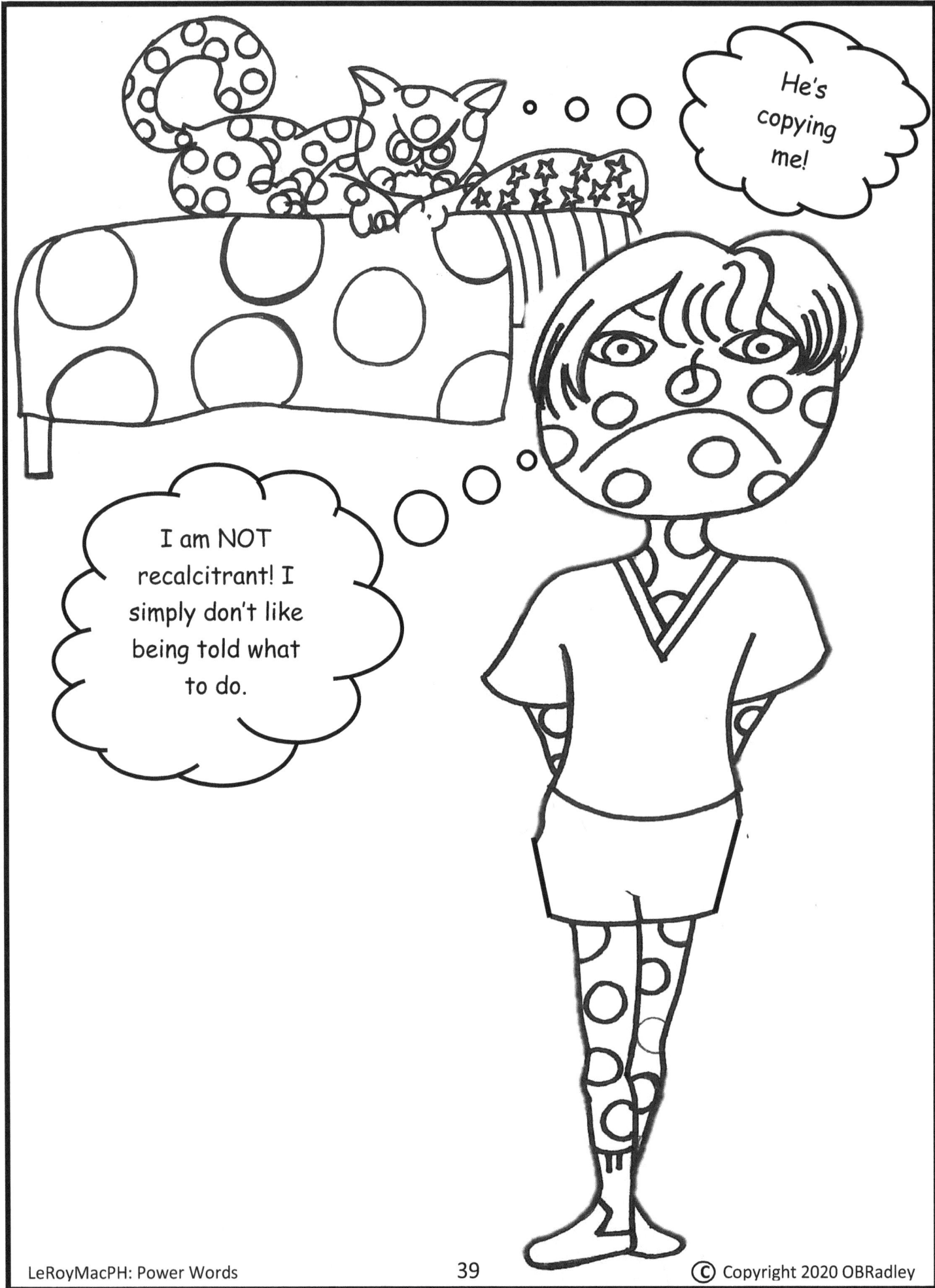

Recalcitrant- stubbornly resistant to authority and control.

(ri-**kal**-si-tr*uh*nt)

- If not for Ryan's <u>recalcitrant</u> attitude, he would have listened to his mother when she warned him not to drink the polkaspot tea.

Noxious- injurious to physical or mental health.

(**nok**-sh*uh*s)

- At 987 years old, Gerald the goldfish finds any activity <u>noxious</u>.

Tangential- of superficial relevance, if any.

Of little value

(tan-**jen**-sh*uh* l)

- Jim often strays down a <u>tangential</u> path of daydreaming while sewing his shirts.

www.ingramcontent.com/pod-product-compliance
Lightning Source LLC
Chambersburg PA
CBHW081232020426
42331CB00012B/3137